THE LONG DISTANCE
RELATIONSHIP GUIDEBOOK

D0913710

THE LONG DISTANCE

RELATIONSHIP GUIDEBOOK:

Strengthen your relationship from afar

Sylvia Shipp

Shipp, Sylvia, 1966-

The Long Distance Relationship Guidebook: Maintain and strengthen your relationship from afar / by Sylvia Shipp. −1st ed.

ISBN: 978-0-6151-3717-9

Designed by Sylvia Shipp

FIRST EDITION

For Mike—my husband and friend.

Acknowledgements

I would like to thank my family, friends, and colleagues for helping me to complete this book. I especially want to thank my tireless husband Mike for helping me with the book theme and editing. I also want to thank my wonderful and resourceful friend Takae for assisting me with surveys and organizing contacts. Finally, I want to express my gratitude to the hundreds of students at Monterey Institute in Monterey, California and to my work colleagues at the UAE University in Al Ain, UAE who generously gave their time and energy to confide in me their thoughts and feelings about their current and past long-distance relationships through countless surveys and interviews.

CONTENTS

PART I INTRODUCTION: PACK YOUR BAGS   1

1. Prepare for your journey: Who needs this book   1

PART II PRE-BOARDING: TAXI THE RUNWAY   7

2. Airsickness: 5 disadvantages of having an LDR   7

3. Flight perks: 11 advantages of having an LDR   13

4. Check your bags: 8 key elements to success   17

5. Boarding: 3 discussions you must have before parting 23

PART III MID-FLIGHT: STAY ON COURSE   31

6. Departure: 9 steps you should take at departure   31

7. Ascent: Gift ideas to make your partner soar   39

8. Layover: Making a temporary visit   51

9. Turbulence: 6 serious LDR problems   57

10. In-flight refueling: Recovering from a break-up   65

PART IV APPROACH: NEARING THE LANDING STRIP   73

11. Cruising altitude: Harmonize your moments   73

12. In-flight meal: Nurture the old-fashioned way   81

13. Duty-free shopping: Bond with simple technology   89

14. In-flight entertainment: Use high-technology   97

PART V DESCENT: SAFE IN THE LOADING DOCK   113

15. A smooth landing: Epilogue   113

About the author   117

THE LONG DISTANCE RELATIONSHIP GUIDEBOOK:

Strengthen your relationship from afar

Part I Introduction: Pack Your Bags

1. Prepare for your journey: Who needs this book

Ladies and gentlemen, flight LDR 123 will soon be boarding. Please have your passport and boarding pass in hand.

Every loving person deserves to be in a meaningful relationship. It seems that when we are not in a relationship, we are forever seeking that special someone who will add meaning to our existence. We strive to find someone who understands, cares, and feels passionate about us and life.

Sometimes we are lucky enough to find Mr. or Mrs. Right, but fate throws in a little twist of her own—one of you must move thousands of miles away, forcing you to make a serious decision to either join your mate, break up, or venture forward in your long distance relationship (LDR) until you are reunited.

Now more than ever, couples need the kind of practical, straightforward advice that is found in *The Long Distance Relationship Guidebook*. The number of long distance relationships continues to grow each year as more men and women accept overseas jobs and studies. At the same time, flights and modes of communication have become more affordable and convenient, making it easier to begin an LDR, but not necessarily easier to stay together.

Even though long distance relationships have become more common, they are still difficult to maintain because of their special circumstances. First of all, long distance relationships are not static, even though at times it may feel like your relationship has been in limbo indefinitely. All the while you are apart, your goals, needs, and desires are constantly changing. Misperceptions about the status of your relationship and each other can arise if you do not update each other regularly on all the changes, small and large, in your lives.

Another reason why LDRs are difficult to sustain is the inherent lack of a physical dimension in your relationship. An otherwise solid relationship can break down when the physical dimension is missing. A relationship lacking a physical dimension can make a person feel detached and lost which can lead to depression. In turn, these feelings of alienation and depression could possibly lead to destructive behavior such as infidelity that could damage the relationship. *The Long Distance Relationship Guidebook* contains discussions and a variety of synchronizing activities that will help you simulate a physical dimension presently lacking in your relationship.

Regularly taking part in these activities will aid you in becoming aware of and preventing absence-related problems *before* they occur. In particular, you may want to check out the synchronized activities in the Cruising altitude chapter.

The Long Distance Relationship Guidebook is an accumulation of insight and practical information collected from interviews and surveys I conducted for over a decade on people involved in long distance relationships. The decision to write this book came about after becoming involved in my own seven-year long distance relationship. During that time, my partner and I were experiencing communication breakdowns and emotional hardships due to the lengthy stretches of time we spent apart from each other.

The few other LDR couples we knew at that time were having similar troubles as well. Although we were able to share our experiences with those other couples, there was a lack of practical information available that pinpointed problems and offered concrete solutions.

The Long Distance Relationship Guidebook is the definitive book on maintaining and strengthening your long distance relationship. This book is intended for couples who have already had time to establish their connection and are now facing the challenge of spending both time and distance apart. At the same time, *The LDR Guidebook* may also benefit those couples who started their relationship off on a less than solid footing. However, whether you are young or old, male or female, or single or married, there is something in this book for all couples involved in LDRs who are interested in turning this challenging time into a passionate and enriching experience.

The mission of this book is to help make this experience while you are apart as successful and comfortable as possible. With *The Long Distance Relationship Guidebook* in hand, learn what you can do to strengthen, nurture, and protect your relationship. Let this book guide you through the rough spots in your relationship, help you foresee problems before they arise, and inspire you to create some wonderful moments for each other. Take part in the activities with your partner, and attempt making use of the gift ideas for the simple reason that, whether we are living together or far apart, we need to know that our significant other is thinking of us. My wish is that your long distance relationship not only overcomes all the challenges and obstacles that lay in your path, but also thrives with hope, love, and passion.

If you are emotionally brave enough to venture forward, and I assume you are or you wouldn't be reading this introduction, then stow your tray table in the upright position and prepare to embark on one of the most rewarding journeys you'll ever take in your life.

Case study: John, businessman

Soon after I graduated from college, I was hired by a company to work on a project in China for five years. My girlfriend and I decided to continue our relationship because we liked each other (and were the marrying type) even though this meant we would spend five years apart. We rarely visited each other and communicated only by letters and phone the whole time, dating other people off and on.

My advice to someone in an LDR would be to make a decision early on and stick to it. If you decide to commit to your partner, be loyal. If not, break away clean for both your sakes. No matter what, be kind and respectful to each other in all circumstances. Don't do anything you would later regret.

In the end, we knew we had to be married if we wanted to stay together, so we got married when I returned from China.

Part II Pre-boarding: Taxi the Runway

2. Airsickness: 5 disadvantages of having an LDR

Ladies and gentlemen, before taking off please familiarize yourself with safety equipment and procedures.

Existing in a long distance relationship with a loved one brings new meaning to the sense of feeling 'lost.' Like many people in long distance relationships, you may find yourself drowning in feelings of loneliness, jealousy, and doubt. Ironically, the time to focus on is not the dimly lit future in which you will reunite. Rather, the time to focus on is now, and what you can do now to make the best of your situation. Now is the time to gather your strength and courage, and direct your energy toward making positive contributions to your partner before your negative feelings take control of you. Be resourceful during this time you are separated from your partner.

Protect your relationship by redirecting negative energy into positive thoughts and behaviors that will improve the quality of your relationship as well as your own mental and emotional well-being. As a result, you will become even more appealing to your partner.

Cultivate positive energy by indulging in your partner. Become an indispensable partner by making him or her feel special and happy to be in a relationship with you. Make this time you are apart an exciting experience by funneling all of your emotional and creative energy toward your partner. You can do all this by taking part in many of the activities listed further along in this book.

Although sadness and restlessness may overwhelm you right now, another way to cultivate positive energy is to look at this time as a chance to enhance your personal life. Spend this time apart by fine-tuning your health and exploring new and exciting interests. Become someone you would greatly admire and enjoy being with.

Below are the five disadvantages that LDR couples tend to mention most often. Each drawback is followed by a few simple suggestions for transforming negative energy into positive energy. Further along in the book, we will see specific examples for diminishing the potential destructiveness of each drawback.

5 disadvantages of being in an LDR

Disadvantage #1: Loneliness

The pain caused by missing each other is often unbearable. How are you supposed to function with this kind of heartache? The following items are general tips of what you can do to ward off feelings of loneliness.

- Take part in activities that simulate a physical dimension.

- Express appreciation for each other in a variety of creative ways.

- Make each moment count whether together or apart.

- Be emotionally brave enough to say when you are having a rough time being apart, and that perhaps you need to visit him or her if possible.

Disadvantage #2: Stress

Some insecurity about your relationship is warranted considering the circumstances. However, left unchecked, worrying about cheating and fear of abandonment can eventually harm both of you. Although these kinds of misfortunes can occur even to couples who live together, make a pact that you will strive to prevent such an unfortunate ending from happening in your LDR using the following measures.

- Maintain an open line of communication.

- Clarify your expectations for every aspect in your relationship.

- Fail-proof your LDR by contributing as much positive energy as possible.

- Take care of your mental and emotional health. Keep yourself busy with things you enjoy doing so that you remain a positive influence.

- Believe in your commitment. Renew your intentions or any vows you have taken occasionally.

Disadvantage #3: Doubt

It's normal and healthy to question whether your partner and relationship is right for you, to a degree. Below are some questions you may want to ask yourself regarding your partner and relationship. For now, go ahead and ask yourself the following questions:

- Would your relationship be stronger if you lived together?

- Do you like, admire, and respect your mate?

- Does he or she bring out the best in you?

- Do you like who you are as a result of being involved with this person, whether physically together or apart?

- Does he or she bring any joy to your life whether near or far?

Disadvantage #4: Awkward reunions

Most couples experience an awkward transitional stage after spending a long time apart, but this does not mean that something is wrong with your relationship. Rather, it may just mean that some time is needed to readjust. Here are a couple of suggestions of things you can do to make your reunions go more smoothly.

- Use humor and talk openly about any uneasiness you are anticipating or experiencing.

- Share a journal during the time you are apart and together so you know exactly what is on each other's minds.

Disadvantage #5: High costs

An LDR is always more expensive in the beginning with regard to phone and transportation costs, even though generally speaking these expenses have decreased over the years. Here are two suggestions for offsetting high costs of maintaining an LDR.

- Write a letter, postcard, or email every day. By communicating your daily events through letters, you can reduce the stress that comes from trying to relay the latest news in a limited amount of time, and in turn increase the amount of play and romantic time spent on the phone.

- Be resourceful. What is your idea of the perfect LDR? How can you turn this sad time apart into a fun, romantic, and even exciting experience? There are a variety of ways to show your love besides phoning or visiting which you will soon see.

Case study: Patty, ballet dancer

My boyfriend and I had a six-year LDR. We saw each other two days a month and spoke everyday on the phone, which cost us each $200 a month. I felt isolated from everyone else. My friends didn't know my partner and couldn't relate to my situation.

The most difficult thing for me was the emotional stress—LDRs are exhausting whether you realize it or not. If you don't know when the separation will end, the fear and uncertainty is draining. But I've always believed that LDRs can work. They're special because these couples don't take each other for granted. It's such an act of love to forego all the wonderful things that you normally get in a relationship that it gives a deeper meaning to the relationship.

Once my boyfriend graduated, we married and moved to NY. All along, I knew that we would get married—otherwise, why else continue the long distance chapter?

3. Flight perks: 11 advantages of having an LDR

Ladies and gentlemen, enjoy your LDR Airlines benefits including non-expiring miles and access to regular news updates.

Your involvement in this long distance phase of your relationship may be a blessing in disguise, in that you have the opportunity to reshape your existing relationship into something grander, or if your relationship is new, start your relationship on the right foot.

Taking advantage of the many benefits that lay at your feet is the first step toward strengthening your long distance relationship.

On the next page is a list of eleven advantages that may help to put you in a better frame of mind about your LDR.

11 advantages of being in an LDR

Self-enrichment

- The extra time you have is an excellent opportunity to focus on your endeavors such as studies, work, and projects.

- Now that you are on your own for a while, indulge in your friendships, hobbies, and sports without feeling neglectful toward your mate.

- If your LDR is new, and you tend to merge passionately with your partners, then this time apart is the perfect chance for you to develop your identity and interests without the influence of a partner in close proximity.

- LDRs can be very exciting. Enjoy the adventures that come with being in one, such as traveling and meeting new people during your visits.

- This may be a good time to negotiate sticky issues over long letters with your partner.

- This is a great chance to hone your romantic letter writing skills and gift making talents.

Creating a stronger bond

- This can be a fun opportunity to get to know each other even better. Right now you have more time to reflect and probe each other a little more with questions and discussions via letters and email.

- Now that you are apart, take this time to focus on important goals you have set for yourself and for you as a couple.

- Let's say there are patterns that have emerged in your current relationship that need improvement. Use this time apart as a chance for a fresh start as to how you relate to each other. Strive to rebuild your relationship into the kind of relationship that both of you want and need.

- Distance lets us step back from the everyday chaos that occurs in a relationship and helps us appreciate its existing strong points. For example, one of the noticeable common strengths in LDRs is the ability to overcome difficult obstacles during separation.

- This is a great time to recount all the wonderful things you do for each other and how much you mean to each other. Use this time to show your appreciation for each other in many different ways.

Case study: Robert, writer

My girlfriend and I were in 4-year LDR. I was in California and she was in her homeland Spain. During that time, we wrote a lot of letters and phoned each other every week.

There are several qualities LDR couples should have including patience, integrity, commitment, a sense of humor, and a strong feeling of love and affection for the other person.

Maintaining a relationship from afar means that you must do all the things that make a great relationship under any circumstances. That means focusing your energy on each other and loving that person unconditionally. You must also like the person for who he or she is, not just as a casual partner who you might go out with now and then. The relationship must transcend the physical. Sex is not an issue, but many non-LDRs are centered on that and I think it gets in the way.

Our relationship culminated in marriage after I finished my studies and my fiancé moved to California.

4. Check your bags: 8 key elements to success

Ladies and gentlemen, please read the following Travel Advisories before boarding the LDR aircraft.

Travel Advisory #1: 5 key compatibility elements

Studies have shown that the chance of a relationship succeeding increases when couples share certain common traits and background factors. Below is a list of five key elements with some examples. Which of the following five key elements or examples in Travel Advisory #1 do you imagine could cause problems for your LDR? Which elements do the both of you value the most as individuals? Which elements do you think connect you as a couple?

5 key compatibility elements

Key element #1: Personality characteristics

Bold people often attract shy people, and creative people sometimes attract intellectual types, but how long can the attraction last if the couple shares little else in common within this key element? Bonds strengthen as couples realize they share the following characteristics:

Examples: Intellect, humor, creativity, sensitivity, sense of adventure, thoughtfulness, health consciousness, reliability, kindness, attractiveness, and libido or sexual style.

Key element #2: Background

Sometimes tension surfaces in a relationship when a couple has had completely different childhood experiences. For example, if one person has had a rough childhood, and the other has been raised in a healthy nurturing environment, they may have different attitudes about how to resolve problems in their relationship or life. Sometimes the differences in childhood experiences are so wide that mutual understanding is nearly impossible on many important issues.

Examples: Childhood experiences, socioeconomic class, education, world view, ethnicity, and religion.

Key element #3: Goals

If you plan on being together in the future, then you should want to end up in the same place. The following are important goals that couples should agree on. It's normal for a partner's goals such as career or education to change a little over time, but ultimately your plans should include the presence of each partner. Obviously, it's a real problem if some goals clash, such as when the couple can't agree on their ultimate home location.

Examples: Education, family building, career, travel, home base, lifestyle, and financial management.

Key element #4: Values

Like goals, it is essential that couples share the same values. Relationships tend to be more successful when both partners share the same values with a similar amount of intensity.

Examples: Honesty, faithfulness, kindness, patience, work ethic, romance, generosity, curiosity, social skills, and moral integrity.

Key element #5: Interests

Less pressing than goals and values, but still important are the interests you are able to share with each other. Enough interests should overlap so that you can relate to each other. If you don't share any interests, then you should try to cultivate some interests you can enjoy together, or at least appreciate each other's differing interests.

Examples: Music, sports, arts, politics, traveling, and hobbies.

Case study: Midori, 25 years old

My boyfriend left Japan a year ago to attend chef school in Paris. Since then I have only visited him once for two weeks. I will finish my studies in California in two years and return to Japan, but my boyfriend hasn't decided if he will return to Japan. So, we aren't sure about our future right now. If he decides to stay in France much longer, it would be hard to continue our relationship.

I think our love is more important than allowing too much time to pass. However, maybe it's the Japanese way, but something holds me back from asking him if I should join him in France. I'm afraid of interrupting his studies, but I am also afraid that I might lose him. I know I need to make a decision on how to handle this soon, but I'm afraid of scaring him off.

Travel Advisory #2: 3 key background dangerous differences

Do you have very different cultures or backgrounds? If so, are you having problems understanding each other's point of view in discussions? Below are three key dangerous background differences that tend to cause problems in relationships. Consider how many background factors you and your partner have in common.

Which of the following background differences in Travel Advisory #2 do you imagine could upset your LDR? Which factors do the both of you value the most as individuals? Which background factors do you think could connect or disrupt you as a couple?

5 key dangerous background differences

Key difference #1: Religious & ethnic

The differences in religious and ethnic orientation may not matter until you must meet each other's family and friends, or until marriage becomes a consideration. For some couples, the need for a mate to have a particular orientation is top priority, especially when it comes to dealing with gender roles, as well as agreeing on marital and parental issues. For other couples, a similar orientation guarantees a better mutual understanding and similar world view.

Key difference #2: Language

Along with religious and ethnic orientation comes a language barrier. Misunderstandings occur even when couples share the same native language. It's hard enough to say how you feel about a complicated emotional issue in your own language, but then when you try explaining yourself in a different language, communication can become a real challenge. To avoid frustration and misunderstandings, use confirmation checks to guide your discussions, such as, "You just said X; by that do you mean Y?"

Key difference #3: Romantic Values

According to research conducted by Dr. Jankowiak, professor and author of *Romantic Passion: The Universal Experience?*, all cultures experience romance, but not all cultures value romance as highly as western cultures do. Generally speaking, other cultures tend to be more pragmatic when it comes to marital issues.

Case study: Ethnic orientation

As an East Indian-American raised in England, Vijay believed that his future wife should have a balanced western and eastern orientation like himself. He believed that finding such a woman would ensure a similar world view and thus a better understanding between them.

5. Boarding: 3 discussions you must have before parting

Ladies and gentlemen, please read the special instructions card located by your seat.

B efore parting, make sure you leave some time to discuss the following three discussion topics. Reaching an agreement on these topics will help to ensure that your intentions and devotion level to each other match closely.

3 essential discussions you should have

Discussion #1: Set up communication guidelines

Most people are not aware of how much of each mode of contact (such as phoning, emailing, or letters) they need to feel comfortable or connected with their partner until they are apart.

To ensure a smooth journey for your upcoming time apart, create a set of communication guidelines together that address your unique circumstances. Establishing guidelines together beforehand are especially helpful in preventing resentment from building up, or preventing disappointments from occurring, such as when someone gets hurt over a perceived long-awaited reply to a letter or email.

Below are some aspects to consider while making your communication guidelines for phoning and emailing. Take into account special circumstances, for example, if one of you is traveling or attending a party, an earlier contact might be desired.

Phoning and email

Below are a few pertinent phoning and email guidelines to agree on before parting.

- How often, on which days, or at what time you should contact each other.

- The maximum amount of time allowed to pass before the other should reply.

- The minimum times per week or month you should contact each other.

Men expressing emotions

According to a number of surveys I conducted, a general pattern emerged regarding men and their seeming lack of awareness about expressing emotions from afar. Indeed, in many of the surveys, both men and women commented on how men unintentionally took their partners for granted. Even though they may have the best intentions, men may not be as emotionally aware as most women are.

Unfortunately, neither partner may realize the extent of his emotional unawareness until after parting ways for a couple of reasons. First, in close proximity, women generally tend to project their own emotions onto their partners. Second, many men may be affectionate when they are with their partner, ironically masking their inability to articulate thoughts and feelings about their relationship.

Sharing a routine every day may make it seem less urgent for men to express themselves emotionally, as many men often innocently view their presence as proof of their love. As a result, men may simply not know how to show feelings when it comes time to separate, and consequently women may experience doubt and disappointment about their partner's apparent negligent behavior.

Case study: Patty, ballet dancer

> The most important aspect of being in an LDR is being involved in and informed of each other's day-to-day life. Couples must share the details of each other's day-to-day life, including the bad and good, so that the relationship remains integral to each other's life.

Discussion #2: Define your boundaries

Every couple should tailor a clear set of dating rules that fit to their particular needs and circumstances. For example, despite some couple's love for each other, they may decide to date while apart. Some such couples use the "Don't ask—don't tell" policy, meaning that if asked, then the other is honor bound to tell the truth. However, if the partner doesn't ask, then it means the partner assumes there is no reason to assume the partner is dating another person, or that he or she doesn't wish to know at that time.

Fidelity

Normally, when a couple is together, their daily presence is a reminder of their commitment. Even so, there are no guarantees against infidelities in any relationship. Sometimes when a partner feels that the time spent apart has gone on for too long, the relationship becomes vulnerable to outside interference.

Unfortunately, neither party may be aware that they have spent too much time apart is until it is too late. Make a pact to treat each other with at least the same amount of respect and courtesy as you would a best friend in your relationship to ensure no one gets hurt.

Although you can't control each other's actions, there are a few things you can both do to diminish the chances of straying from occurring in your LDR. The following are some examples of a few things you can do. And as before, we'll see more specific examples of the kinds of activities you can do in following chapters.

- Take part in activities that make you both feel loved and special on a daily basis.

- Enrich your lives by pursuing interests, including finding some that you both appreciate. Educate yourselves more about each other's interests.

- Be so special that you become indispensable to each other emotionally, intellectually, spiritually, physically, and sexually.

Discussion #3: Vow to stay plugged in

Some people in LDRs get so consumed with their daily lives that days seem to blur together and they forget to maintain contact. To avoid making your mate feel like he or she is being taken for granted, alert one another of upcoming busy periods. Channel a lot of energy into each other so that you feel plugged in to each other's lives. This means you may need to make more comments and pose more questions about your partner's endeavors in your email and letters to show you are involved in his or her life in an effort to compensate for your absence.

Case study: Justin, computer programmer

My advice for someone in an LDR is that if you love and expect to marry that person, then continue with the relationship. Otherwise, it's not worth it, and maintaining your relationship will be hard on both of you.

My girlfriend and I had been together for four years before we had to separate for two years. We communicated by letters and phone calls, but couldn't visit each other due to lack of funds.

In the end, I screwed things up because I put in minimal effort knowing we wouldn't be together for such a long time. I thought it would just be easiest to break up even though I loved her immensely!

Try the seven Boarding activities on the following page before parting.

7 Boarding activities

1. Journal

Keeping a daily journal of your thoughts and feelings about your significant other is a great way to deal with the emotional stress of being in an LDR. It gives you a private place to vent frustrations and reflect on the challenges you are currently facing in your relationship.

2. Swap shop

Exchange lucky charms, photos, baby pictures, and love letters that you can carry around with you while you are apart.

3. Tandem effort

Before your mate leaves, write a postcard or letter together. The happy memories of your last days together will be all that much brighter when the postcard arrives in the mailbox.

4. Planner

Before parting, decorate a calendar for each other with encouraging words and drawings to commemorate important dates. Your new personalized calendar will make you think of your partner every time you gaze at it.

If you are apart for long stretches at a time, make a calendar based on a variety of twelve photos of you together and send each other copies. Choose photos that correspond with the seasons.

5. Letter surprise

One of the sweetest things you can do is secretly write and send a love letter before your partner returns home from his or her visit with you. The first day apart is usually the saddest, and what better pick-me-up is there (outside of making a surprise appearance) than to have a love letter waiting in the mailbox?

6. Pack it up

After your partner has finished packing, enclose love notes and pictures throughout his or her suitcase, in the pockets of clothing, toiletry bag, and purse or wallet. Hide some notes well so that even days later, he or she continues to find loving messages from you.

7. Symbol

Create your own secret correspondence symbol. For example, one couple drew the Hopi sun symbol on all their letters and envelopes. To them, the sun symbol represented the four pillars that their relationship was based on, namely love, friendship, respect, and fidelity.

Part III Mid-flight: Stay On Course

6. Departure: 9 steps you should take at departure

Ladies and gentlemen, fasten your seat belt and make sure your seat back and folding trays are in their full upright position.

As you part, and immediately afterwards, there is still work to be done to make sure that your relationship stays on course. On the following pages are nine steps you should take during and immediately after your departure to keep your relationship on track.

9 steps to take during and after departure

Step #1: Leave a positive impression

Consider what lasting image you want to imprint on your partner when it is time to say goodbye, considering that this will be the last image your partner will have of you for many weeks or months to come. With this in mind, choose the outfit that he or she likes best on you. Also, make sure you have enough tissues on hand in case either of you breaks down.

Step #2: Remain open

Sometimes the fear of having to part hastens a couple to move along faster then it normally would. Promises made under pressure or out of desperation make it difficult for couples to assess at what point they really are in their romantic development. Be open with your feelings and thoughts if you think your relationship is progressing too swiftly. Rather than promise too much out of desperation or to assuage your partner's fears, it's better in the long run to simply say less and hold each other close before parting.

Step #3: Work toward better understanding

Effective and honest communication means what you say, how you say it, and when you say it. In LDRs, misunderstandings are often caused by hasty email writing, a language barrier, differing expectations of feelings or behavior, and an inability to articulate thoughts and feelings. Make an effort to hone your writing and phone skills so that your mate feels your warm presence whether near or far.

Case study: Miscommunication

As a university student in England, Wesley met a young woman during summer camp. They lived five hours away from each other, making it difficult to see each other more than twice a month. She was his ideal woman, as well as his first girlfriend. Although they had broken up before, it came as a surprise when she abruptly ended their relationship. Too young and immature to articulate her doubts and fears, she gave mixed messages toward the end of their relationship. Young and inexperienced, Wesley also lacked a solid awareness of his own feelings. In the end, their breakup crushed him and he found it difficult to open up emotionally for many years afterward.

Step #4: Stick to the familiar

As a result of inherent time restrictions, some new LDRs develop rather quickly, resulting in even the smallest things magnifying in significance. Passionate greetings and farewells intensify the focus as well, increasing expectations of each other and the next reunion. Make an effort to discuss mundane issues to stay connected at a familiar level. Acknowledge changing needs, goals, interests, and influences, as well as changes in resources like time and money.

Step #5: Interweave the emotional fabric

You must put forth a lot of energy weaving each other into your daily life, especially in the beginning. During this time of physical absence is a great opportunity to focus on each other's emotional needs. Maintain an ongoing emotional dialog so that you talk openly about issues that matter to you the most.

Step #6: Portray yourself honestly

Sometimes distance blurs the lines between reality and illusion. Make a commitment to portraying yourselves honestly. If your relationship is new, learn more about each other by acquainting yourselves with each other's family and friends. Probe each other's character more deeply by asking revealing questions from a relationship-building question book.

Step #7: Create a physical dimension

It is essential that you simulate a physical dimension to offset each other's absence. You can do this in several ways. One way is by surrounding yourself with items such as the photos, letters, maps, clothing articles, and personal items of your significant other.

Another way you can create a physical dimension is by synchronizing the moments of your daily rituals. For example, you can coordinate when and what you watch on TV, when and what kind of music you listen to, and when and what clothes you wear to school or work. We will see many more examples of these kinds of activities that nurture a physical sense of togetherness in the upcoming Cruising altitude chapter. Finally, you can make simple gifts tailored to each other's uniqueness. Engaging in these different types of bonding activities will help you feel closer even though you may be many miles apart.

Step #8: Safeguard your LDR

Worrying about cheating is one of the most emotionally draining disadvantages about being in a long distance relationship since you are at the mercy of each other's moral integrity. If you are concerned about protecting your LDR from outside interference, then agree to take the following steps together to safeguard your relationship.

- Take precaution at social situations such as parties, especially if you are suffering from loneliness or currently holding a grudge against your mate.

- Be wary of weaknesses you might have that could sabotage your relationship, such as the inability to handle alcohol or attention from an attractive member of the opposite sex.

- Take care with flirting. Some people argue that in general, men are not as used to flattery and attention as women are, and may therefore be more vulnerable to seduction.

- As a fundamental rule, do not do anything that you wouldn't do if your mate were present.

Case study: 24-hour courtesy warning

Rob and Nora were a new couple when Nora was hired as a researcher in Austria for a year. Meanwhile, Rob was still coming to terms with a recently ended relationship. As a result, they were unsure of each other's level of commitment when it came time for Nora to leave.

Out of respect for each other and to avoid the pain of infidelity, they made a pact to give a 24-hour courtesy warning if one of them were about to become sexually involved with someone else. However, this warning functioned more as a psychological buffer to prevent unnecessary worrying rather than a statement that they planned on cheating. Luckily, they never had to use the courtesy warning, but it relieved them of having to worry about being betrayed.

Step #9: Know your limits

Draw your mate closer to you by wearing a personal item belonging to him or her before attending a social gathering, especially if you are feeling lonely, depressed, or if you tend to flirt while drinking. Wear or take an intimate object belonging to or associated with him or her such as tee shirt or socks, a piece of jewelry, or some cologne. You can also carry around a photo and the most recent letter or postcard you have received from your partner.

Alternatively, you could turn your watch to your mate's time zone or carry a compass (with a notch etched into it so that it's pointing toward his or her direction). Look at your partner's photo before leaving the house and talk to it. Say where you are going and what time you plan to return home. Place another picture of him or her on your pillow before leaving your house for the evening.

Case study: Know your limitations

During the year they spent apart, Nora knew she had a drinking problem, but hadn't yet reached the point of knowing she needed to quit drinking. Before leaving for Austria, as a preventative measure against straying while drinking, she recycled one of Rob's underwear bands to wear around her waist to serve as a reminder of her commitment to him. She viewed her innovative safety measure with a mixture of seriousness and humor in her earnest effort to remain faithful when she would be drinking in social gatherings.

Try the three Departure activities on the following page immediately after parting.

3 Departure activities

1. Write a pre-farewell letter

Parting is such a stressful time that it can make us act withdrawn or strange when it comes time to say goodbye. Channel your emotions into a letter to your partner before your final day together approaches. Write down your feelings, thoughts, dreams, and fears and let him or her read the letter before parting. Releasing some emotions beforehand may help you feel more composed, and thus enable you to give more of yourself emotionally to your partner on the farewell day, leaving him or her with an inspiring final impression of you.

2. Write a post-farewell letter

After your mate leaves, don't just sit there feeling sick with sadness. This is the perfect time to sit somewhere quiet and write a love letter, listing all the reasons why you love and admire him or her. Mail it immediately so that it arrives soon after your mate's arrival to his or her destination.

3. Send more warm greetings

Along with writing a postcard or letter just before or immediately after your partner returns home from a visit with you, have an answering machine message and an email waiting for him or her.

7. Ascent: Gift ideas to make your partner soar

Ladies and gentlemen, our flight attendants are coming around with magazines and newspaper carts for your reading enjoyment.

Gifts do not have to be elaborate or expensive to make your partner feel special. The Ascent chapter shows how you can strengthen your bond by making simple, affordable gifts that are easy to tailor to each other's uniqueness. Whether you are making a gift or engaging in an activity, keep your partner's picture nearby to help you stay focused on the romantic task at hand.

Show your partner how you feel by choosing from the following twenty Ascent gift-making ideas.

20 Ascent gift ideas

1. Find-a-word

Make a word puzzle using words that describe your mate, or clues to where you are going to take him or her on the next visit. There are several sites online where you can create and print your own puzzle.

2. Message puzzle

Find a card shop or craft store that sells blank puzzles for you to paint or write a message on. Send the whole puzzle at one time or a couple of pieces in a letter at a time.

3. City puzzle

Send a commercial made puzzle of a photo of your city or country. Personalize it by pasting your pictures onto two interlocking pieces. Then put the two pieces with your pictures aside in an envelope with instructions to your mate to open the envelope once the puzzle is nearly completed, and place them last into the puzzle.

4. Maps

Mail and pin up each other's city street or country map. Before you mail your map, use a highlighter to mark the location of your house.

When you have each other's maps pinned up, stick a pin into your mate's highlighted area.

5. Resolutions

Share your New Year's resolutions, even if it's not January 1st. Discuss short- and long-term goals, personality qualities you want to work on, or habits you want to change. Make resolutions that entail as many of your qualities as possible, including physical, emotional, intellectual, and creative.

6. 'Tis the season

Send natural gifts that showcase your environment, especially if you live in different climates. For example, if you live in a Mediterranean climate, mail a packet of jasmine blossoms. If you live in a colder climate, encase and iron some colorful fall leaves in a sheet of wax paper. In the winter, send dried mistletoe with your picture taped underneath.

Create a scratch and sniff game for each season. For example, in the winter, dab a card with ground up traces of pinecone, incense, candy cane, gingerbread, and spices. Number the items and have your partner guess each smell.

Send a CD compilation of holiday songs sung by your favorite artists. This is nice for nostalgic reasons, and interesting if you speak different languages.

Make and send Christmas tree ornaments from photos, a piece of fabric from the shirt you wore when you first met, a lock of hair, or a miniature painting. Alternatively, make traditional ornaments such as strung dried cranberries.

7. Achtung!

Send a German Advent calendar if you are apart during December. It looks like a thin A4-sized cardboard box with a colorful picture of a house with many window shutters, numbered from one to twenty-five and ending with Christmas day. Each shutter encases a uniquely shaped holiday chocolate. An Advent calendar is a great spirit booster and helps you see that time really *is* passing.

8. Bundle up

Dress your mate according to the season and his or her unique needs. For example, if your partner's feet are always cold, send a pair of warm fuzzy socks with a note saying they will keep them warm until the next visit.

Many stores have online outlets that sell last season's items at a reduced price. Try typing "outlet" as your online store search word. The following items are examples of inexpensive gifts you can send.

- Spring: A fun t-shirt or sporty underwear.

- Summer: A cap, tank top imprinted with your alma mater or city, or flavored lip balm.

- Fall: A scarf, flannel shirt, shawl, or flannel boxers.

- Winter: Thick socks, warm slippers or moccasins, gloves, hat, earmuffs, bathrobe, or pjs.

9. Johnny West

Connect to the part of your mate's life that you missed out on, namely childhood, by re-introducing his or her favorite childhood toy, game, record, or book. Find out what the favorite toy was and buy it on an Internet auction site.

10. Goofball

Bring out the kid in your partner. Send simple toys such as Mattel cars or plastic farm animals. Send a silly toy, such as a paddleball, squirt gun, or silly putty. Or, buy a stuffed animal that fits to your partner's personality.

> I personalize my envelopes to my boyfriend by drawing small pictures on them. I also occasionally write mushy poems and send photos to him. Since he is attending college in a rural place, I send him Top Ramen noodles, other Japanese foods, and silly toys in a care package.

11. Housewarming

If your mate has recently moved, send a traditional housewarming gift according to the ethnic tradition of the country he or she is living in. Or, send something more personal, such as a scented cotton pillowcase or a packet of flower seeds.

12. Hourglass

Send a clear container filled with the same number of small candies such as Hershey's Kisses or Skittles as the number of days you will be apart. Instruct your mate to eat one per day until you see each other again.

13. Swap meet

Wear one of your t-shirts for a day, scent it with your cologne, and send it as a nightshirt gift. Trade slightly worn shirts or sweaters each time you visit.

14. Olé!

Fill a piñata or a small stuffed animal with candy and folded love notes. Or, sew up the goodies in a scented cloth satchel.

Case study: John, businessman

My girlfriend sent me a couple of tape letters of herself talking and even singing. I mailed her a few little trinkets that I picked up during my travels. Once, I gave her a funny-romantic collage of us that I made from old magazines. Sometimes we sent photos to each other of friends, family and ourselves.

15. Treasure chest

Customize a care package to match your partner's unique personality. Choose items from the following five main categories.

Tactile

- A scented teddy bear with a love note.
- Trinkets or jewelry.
- A small gadget or toy.
- An article of clothing.
- A good luck penny or currency from your state or country.

Gustatory

- Freshly baked cookies.
- Coffee or loose tea and tea ball.
- Candy or snacks.
- Gold-wrapped chocolate coins.
- Fortune cookies.
- Hard to find specialty food items.
- Salt and pepper shakers to capture your couple's spirit.
- A personalized coffee cup.

Visual

- A love poem or drawing.
- A recent photo or baby picture.
- Books or magazines.
- News article clippings.
- A CD or DVD.

- A book of word puzzles.

- A Sno-globe ® showcasing your city.

- A romance journal.

- A key chain with compass. Etch or mark with a pen the direction you live in with respect to your mate's location so he or she always knows which direction to look for you.

- A key chain with flashlight for your night-owl partner.

- A customized pen with a message engraved on it.

- A souvenir pen from your city.

- A theme calendar.

- Souvenir placemats or a calendar depicting your city.

- Refrigerator magnets to post notes or postcards.

Aural

- A tape letter.

- A CD music compilation.

- A classic comedy CD.

- An instructional how-to CD.

The back-to-school or work treasure chest

- Soft ear plugs.

- Eye cover.

- A weekly planner.

- Warm socks.

- A compass.

- A fountain pen.

- A medicine chest containing Tums, aspirin, cold and flu medicine, and vitamin C.

- Hard to find food items or toiletries.

- A customized folder decorated with pictures and drawings.

- A fail-proof or novelty alarm clock.

Case study: Thomas, linguistics major

I recently sent my girlfriend in Sweden a care package which included an environmental t-shirt since she is studying ecology. I also sent plastic straws formed into the shape of hearts, as well as a large block of Ghirardelli chocolate and Djarum clove cigarettes. I have given her books on environmental topics, as well as information on studies in the U.S. So far, she has sent me magazines, information on her country, a bell, a piggy bank to save money for my trip out there, and of course, photos and tapes.

16. Good luck charm

Buy inexpensive jewelry that can be worn as a good luck charm. Try searching import specialty shops online to find charms that fit to your partner's origins or interests. On the following page are some examples of good luck charms.

- A necklace with a birthstone or scarab. A scarab is a petrified beetle encased in a semi-precious stone, such as turquoise.
- A Celtic knot bracelet.
- Earrings with an embedded birthstone.
- An old lucky penny, or a shiny new one, especially if you have different currencies.
- A Buddhist blue eye charm.
- A Native-American Indian dream catcher.

17. Love messenger

If you know someone who is about to visit your partner's town, arm your stealthy love messenger with a love letter and a rose to place on his or her doorstep on your behalf.

18. Posey express

Send flowers, chocolate, or a unique gift with a message through an online international company such as FTD or Hershey. If you want to send something different, use search words such as unique or novelty.

19. Headlines

Read your partner's online newspaper including the city's weather forecast. Amuse yourselves by reading each other's daily horoscope. Then send an email later that day to report "how his or her day went."

20. ESPN.com…?

It's likely your partner has interests you know nothing about. Research the hobbies, music, sports, line of work, culture, or college major online. If you are planning to spend the rest of your life with each other, it might be fun (not to mention a nice surprise for your mate) to educate yourself in those interests.

Even seemingly boring hobbies are more interesting after doing a little research on them. For example, if your mate is interested in American football, visit the URL nfl.com. It's just one more thing you will be able to share when you're together one day.

Case study: Robert, writer

One thing my girlfriend and I did that made our relationship special was sending each other unique gifts. For example, when I was visiting Rome, I bought a blessing from the Pope, which is a proclamation on parchment with the Pope's picture, and sent it to her family. She sometimes sent me pictures she had drawn depicting us in humorous situations.

8. Layover: Making a temporary visit

Ladies and gentlemen, take advantage of our LDR frequent flyer VIP lounge. Enjoy the amenities before your connecting flight.

Enduring a rough transition

A t last! You are together, for a while anyway, until one of you must return home to continue working or studying. Layover is a special chapter dedicated to couples who met on holiday or had little time to establish a firm foundation before launching themselves into their LDR, and are now experiencing some confusion or problems. In most cases, couples live in a different city or country, but in many cases, couples live in different countries or even different continents.

Perhaps you noticed during this past visit, the first visit since you met and fell in love, that things felt a little awkward and strange. What has changed? And more importantly, why have things changed?

How much of feeling "right" about each other is based on the setting in which you met, whether you were on holiday, or whether that exhilaration you felt was a result of the kind of excitement that goes along with a burgeoning relationship? Sometimes you have to ask yourself if you were in love with the place and situation, or if you were in love with the person. In the following pages, consider whether any of the typical transitional problems are responsible for causing the friction you may be currently experiencing in your relationship.

Case study: Satoshi, 25 years old

We met in the summer and returned to our hometowns before school started. We were a couple from the beginning even though apart the first nine months. At first, I didn't plan to marry her. We communicated only by letters and telephone.

I think the LDR depends a lot on luck, in that your partner may leave you for someone else, even though things are going well. I think humans are too weak to withstand being apart from each other for a long time. Fortunately, luck has been on my side since I am about to marry the girlfriend I've been in an LDR with.

Getting to know each other again

The first days you spend together during a visit are often a little awkward after having spent months apart, but this is a normal transition and does not necessarily mean that there is anything wrong with your partner or relationship. For each new visit, it takes time to readjust to the new set of circumstances.

However, sometimes things just do not feel right, and you can't quite put your finger on the reason why. Consider whether anything has changed in your environment. Did you meet on holiday? Were you a fun couple at first but are now placed in a serious setting? Were you two alone before, but now are faced with spending a lot of time with family and friends?

The length of time it takes to adjust to the new circumstances depends on the amount of time spent apart, your personalities, and the extent to which your situation has changed.

If you are experiencing a rough transition during your visit, ask yourself whether a sudden presence or absence has occurred in one of the following seven environmental factors.

7 environmental factors that can affect your LDR

1. Setting. Are you basking in a cozy cottage setting like last time, or have you been thrust into a small, noisy apartment?

2. Family. Are you alone with your partner, or are you suddenly surrounded by scores of nosy family members?

3. Friends. Are your friends considerate, or do they add tension to your relationship with their drunken debaucheries?

4. Work. Are you both taking time off at the moment, or is one of you working overtime to beat an important deadline?

5. School. Are you visiting in the summer time, or is one of you finishing projects and cramming for exams?

6. Vacation. Are you on vacation at the moment, or are you both under stress from work and school?

7. Money. Do you have enough money to enjoy simple pleasures, or are you both worried about making ends meet?

Entering the public realm

LDRs usually function smoothly in the initial private stage. However, once family and friends are introduced into the relationship, some couples begin experiencing problems. If an LDR collapses once it is exposed to the outside world, then most likely the relationship wasn't based on a firm foundation to begin with.

Anticipating obstacles

If you are about to visit family and friends for the first time, then be considerate and warn your mate about committing offenses that would prevent him or her from making a good impression. Help your mate to make a good impression by explaining the social situation, beliefs, traditions, expectations, and the idiosyncrasies of each important family member beforehand so that he or she knows what to expect, as well as what is expected of him or her.

Case study: Moving into the public realm

Sarah and Adam fell in love while he was visiting her seaside town on holiday. A few months later, she visited him in Austria where he lived with his parents.

Sarah met his friends, observed his routine, and went sight-seeing. But when his parents returned home from holiday a few days later, Adam became tense and withdrawn. Although his parents had been generous and hospitable as they had bought her a flight ticket and welcomed her in their home, they were also formal and scrutinizing.

Adam was ashamed of his parents' house rules, and reluctant to share them with Sarah. As a result, they viewed her as a rude house guest. After a few tense days, Adam finally informed Sarah of her peccadilloes, and once she began observing the house rules, they were all able to enjoy the rest of her visit.

9. Turbulence: 6 serious LDR problems

Ladies and gentlemen, we are coming into some turbulence. Please return to your seats and keep your seat belts fastened.

Imagine tension-causing problems in your relationship as little monster eggs. If you don't confront them directly, they will hatch and grow into monsters that will wreak havoc on your relationship.

Every problem that arises in your LDR whether you are together or apart is a chance to learn something about yourself and each other. For example, are you emotionally brave when your relationship is having problems? What about morally strong in your partner's absence? Now is a good time to make an honest assessment about yourself and your relationship, as well as your commitment to your partner.

Case study: Setting & background differences

Omar and Laila had just become engaged when she graduated from their university and had to return to her home in Damascus. Before parting, they made a pact to remain faithful.

After two years of excited waiting, Omar visited Laila in her hometown. However, when they met, she was tense and aloof. This continued for the entire length of his visit and Omar returned home confused and broken-hearted. He also felt betrayed and regretted the time he had faithfully waited for her.

While traveling one winter, a freak snowstorm hit and Omar's layover was extended a few days during a chance layover in Damascus. Laila met him at the airport and confessed that she had been ashamed of her family's poverty. As she opened up, Omar could see the lady he had adored and they fell in love again.

In the following pages, examine the six serious relationship problems that many LDR couples must face.

6 serious LDR problems

Serious problem #1: As is

Now that you are apart and have time to reflect on your relationship, do you find yourself spending a lot of time focusing on your partner's shortcomings? Do you feel your partner lacks something you value strongly? If so, could you share this interest with a friend if it is something less integral, such as an interest in politics, or a quality such as a keen intellect? If this lacking involves something more substantial, such as a goal or value, do you feel that you would compromise yourself by overlooking it? In other words, you have to decide whether you would be better off with or without your mate.

Serious problem #2: Constant postponing

Your interests and goals, big or small, keep changing over time. It's great if you can support each other's endeavors even if it means delaying your final reunion a little. But if you keep delaying your reunion time after time, you may want to question whether you have unresolved commitment or intimacy issues.

Serious problem #3: Domicile difficulties

Richard Carlson points out in his self-actualizing book *Don't Sweat the Small Stuff in Love* that we need to allow plenty of time to adapt to major transitions in our life. One of these major transitions in life is adjusting to living together again.

You have been waiting and struggling for months or even years to reunite for the last time. So now that you are finally physically together, why aren't you getting along? Hopefully, this is just a rough phase that you will get through quickly with lots of discussion, patience, and humor.

59

When you were apart and communication was mainly through email, there was no need to respond immediately. Time spent talking on the phone was limited, and your topics probably covered a smaller range due to a lack of time and desire to eliminate extraneous topics from your conversation.

Now that you have reunited, you play a larger role in each other's life. Communication is face-to-face again, covering a wider range of issues from the serious to the mundane. In addition, your partner's behaviors are resurfacing, for better or worse. And last but not least, responsibilities must be redistributed, and routine decisions must be made together again.

Serious problem #4: Know your shelf life

Many good LDRs do not work out even with the best intentions. Consider agreeing upon an expiration date, at which point you acknowledge your relationship is no longer progressing in a way that suits either of your best interests. If one of you reaches the point where you don't want to continue the way things are, then gently let each other know where you stand. Time your conversation thoughtfully to avoid breaking up before an event important to your partner such as an interview or exam.

Serious problem #5: When to call it quits

Maybe you recall the 1996 tragedy on Mount Everest in which many climbers died in a sudden snowstorm while ascending to the top. Every year climbers die on their way to the summit because they fail to read the impending danger signs. Likewise, in an LDR, don't become so goal-oriented in reaching the finish line that you begin ignoring inauspicious signs that your relationship is deteriorating.

Serious problem #6: Red alert warning signs

On the following pages are two lists of red alert warning signs that may signal your long distance relationship is coming to an end, or that your partner wishes to move on or in fact has already moved on with someone else. The first list has signs you may notice in your partner while physically apart, and the second list includes signs you may see in your partner during a visit. As every situation is different, these warning signs are only meant to guide you, so weigh the evidence carefully with your best reasoning and gut feeling before confronting your partner.

17 pre-evacuation red alert warning signs (if physically apart)

Your relationship may be in trouble if your partner…

1. decreases the quality and quantity of contact.
2. makes flimsy excuses for not contacting you.
3. sounds annoyed when you call.

4. makes future plans that don't include you.

5. disagrees with things you once agreed on.

6. is terse and impatient.

7. is antagonistic and condescending.

8. has a sudden general negative outlook.

9. acts emotionally distant.

10. keeps postponing or avoids talking about your next reunion.

11. says there won't be much time for you during your next visit.

And perhaps…

12. develops new tastes in music or clothes.

13. splurges money (that he or she doesn't have) on expensive clothes, hairstyle, makeup, music, or other luxury items.

14. develops radically new interests.

15. becomes involved in a new set of friends.

16. mentions he or she has met an interesting person of the opposite sex.

17. poses a "hypothetical" question about whether it would be okay to pursue an interesting friendship.

11 pre-evacuation red alert warning signs (if physically together)

Your relationship may be in trouble if your partner…

1. is aloof and unaffectionate.

2. is antagonistic and argumentative.

3. acts uncomfortable or strange.

4. hesitates to answer the telephone.

5. answering machine volume is set on lowest setting.

6. doesn't play answering machine openly.

7. wears a new cologne or perfume.

8. has put away your old pictures and memorabilia.

9. has not put up your most recent pictures and memorabilia.

10. has replaced your wallpaper setting picture on his monitor with something impersonal.

11. you find unfamiliar items in his or her house or car such as clothing, hair strands, or gifts.

10. In-flight refueling: Recovering from a break-up

Ladies and gentlemen, in-flight refueling operations are underway which may result in some turbulence. Keep your seatbelt fastened until further notified.

The In-flight refueling chapter is for people who are currently experiencing a break-up and are struggling with the pain of losing their significant other. For better or worse, your involvement with your partner makes you a well-seasoned traveler. This chapter outlines three major positive actions you should take immediately that will help you recover quickly from your breakup in a healthy way.

Case study: Michiko, graduate student

My advice to someone in a long distance relationship is that you should live your own life. We have spent more time apart than together. If during our next visit we still feel the same as before, then we will stay together. People should not forget each other and do their best to stay together, but they should also not expect too much since a lot can happen while you are apart.

4 positive actions to take to heal quickly

Positive action #1: Do your best to make it work

Above all, if you have the misfortune of your LDR coming to an end, do everything in your power to make your relationship work, if in your heart you wish to preserve it. Then if it does end, knowing you did your best will give you some peace of mind and help you move on. If you neglect to mend this relationship while the chance still exists, it may haunt you for a long time afterwards with thoughts of what you should have done.

Positive action #2: Treat yourself right

Imagine it is one year from now and you are looking back at how you conducted yourself. How do you wish you had handled yourself? Does it match with how you are handling things now?

Neglecting yourself, getting drunk, or other forms of self-imposed abuse after a bad breakup will only postpone the healing process. Instead, imagine that you are your own best friend. What course of action would you prescribe to help your best friend recover from such an emotional crisis?

Positive action #3: Take the driver's seat

To speed up your quick recovery, take control of your life now before your breakup takes control of you. It may be hard to imagine today, but somehow everything really *will* be all right. Channel your pain into positive actions that will help forge the rebirth of your new stronger self. Think of this time not as the end of something, but as the beginning of something else.

Many loving people have been lucky enough to find themselves in more than just one loving relationship. Appealing opportunities will find their way into your life again. You can prepare yourself for that moment by taking care of yourself and tending to your interests, so that when that person does cross your path, you will be ready for him or her. Below you will find fourteen emotional and seven physical steps some people have taken to recover from their painful breakups.

Positive action #4: Do what you need to heal properly

There are many bold emotional, physical, mental, and spiritual steps you need to take if you wish to heal yourself in a healthy way within a reasonable amount of time. Out of convenience, these steps have been categorized into two primary groups: emotional and physical.

14 emotional steps you should take to heal quickly

1. Grieve and vent in a journal.

2. Vent your emotions in letters or email to your ex-partner that you do not send.

3. Write well-thought out letters or email that you hold onto and edit for many days or weeks before sending. If possible, have an honest friend read it first before sending.

4. Meditate or visualize positive thoughts and images of yourself and record them in your journal.

5. Express your pain creatively through art. A friend of mine painted a picture of his ex-girlfriend from a photo to help him get her out of his system.

6. Surround yourself with supportive friends who are good listeners. The more you talk, the faster you will process the pain and come to terms with your breakup.

7. Spend light-hearted time with good, funny friends.

8. Watch non-romance comedies. Research studies have shown that laughing raises serotonin levels, giving you a sense of well-being.

9. Remove the photos and renovate your room. You must build new memories now.

10. Boldly revisit places where you once spent time together. You are building new memories now which will eventually replace the old painful ones.

11. Take a brave step in getting your LDR behind you by announcing in a brief group email to family and friends that your relationship is over.

12. Do not be ashamed about your misfortune. Everyone suffers a heart wrenching breakup at some point in his or her life.

13. Keep yourself busy by doing good things for others and yourself. Volunteer for a cause or join a club, such as a hiking group or a writing circle.

14. Reinvent yourself. How can you improve your life physically, spiritually, mentally, creatively, and emotionally? Write a recovery plan that discusses where you wish to be in three months, six months, and one year from now.

7 physical steps you should take to heal quickly and completely

1. Eat healthy food and take vitamins. The emotional anguish caused by the breakup puts your mind and body in a vulnerable state right now.

2. Exercise. Use an MP3 player to keep your mind focused. Listen to instructional or inspirational material rather than indulging in heartbreak music.

3. Get weekly massages to help you heal and relax. Check beauty schools for affordable rates.

4. Heal from the outside inward by treating yourself to a facial or new (but not outrageous) hair style.

5. Avoid alcohol and dating until you have regained composure over your thoughts, feelings, and behavior.

6. Take antacids to ease the stomach acid.

7. If you having severe problems sleeping or working, consult your doctor about getting a small prescription of tranquilizers to see you through the first few days of intense grieving.

Case study: A quick recovery

As a young woman, Nicki had a significant relationship that ended abruptly. She called her mother crying on the phone and told her all about it. After listening to Nicki, her mother told her to go straight to the store and fill a cart full of healthy food and juice. Her words sounded corny at first, but Nicki took her advice at a crucial point following her breakup.

Soon afterwards, she realized what a powerful self-affirming message she had given herself by treating herself well. By following her mother's advice, Nicki was able to steer clear of self-destructive behavior and get on the road to recovery more quickly.

Part IV Approach: Nearing the Landing Strip

11. Cruising altitude: Harmonize your moments

Ladies and gentlemen, we have reached cruise altitude at 36,000 feet. Please feel free to get up and move around the cabin.

Even though distance separates you physically, it is essential that you attempt to synchronize your daily routines along with special moments to maintain a sense of familiarity and immediacy that is normally found in most healthy relationships. The Cruising altitude chapter will show you how to achieve this.

Synchronize your routine with activities

Many of the following seventeen Cruising altitude activities require that they are done simultaneously. Try to synchronize as many of your daily rituals as possible so that you are doing the same activities at the same moment. However, if the time zone difference is too great and this prevents the possibility for overlapping your routines, then conduct your activities according to your respective time zones. For example, watch the same film when it is 8pm Friday for each of you, respectively. If this is also too strenuous due to busy schedules, then allow your activities to unfold within the same week.

The following are some fun and romantic examples of how you and your partner can synchronize your routine.

8 visual and aural activities

1. Watch a designated film on the same night of the week at the same time while eating the same snacks.

2. Listen to a designated CD or song on certain days or times while doing the same activities.

3. Coordinate a reading of the same book, magazine, or online newspaper. At bedtime, read the same humorous book so that you know you are both laughing out loud at the same time.

4. Play online interactive games or cruise through the same chat rooms at the same time. Yahoo offers a variety of multi-player online games that couples can play together.

5. Designate your own constellation or star for both of you to gaze at together every evening.

6. While phoning each other, look at the moon or the same constellation, if possible.

7. Display the same wallpaper image as your screensaver.

8. Keep matching calendars.

6 physical activities

1. Dress similarly on designated days so that you wear the same color shirts or tennis shoes.

2. Keep to the same weekly dinner menu as if you were living together. Eat the same meals on the same nights of the week.

3. Wear a watch that keeps each other's local time.

4. Buy the same scented or flavored items you use daily, such as toothpaste, body wash, shampoo, lip balm, and breath mints.

5. Drink the same beverage out of the same style coffee mug.

6. Use the same style key chain, mouse pad, or pen.

3 spiritual activities

1. Write your journal entry at the same time.

2. Meditate on each other at a designated time each day for one minute.

3. Watch time pass together at the same time. Buy a long candle for each of you. With a knife, section off the candle according to the number of weeks or months you will be apart with shallow notches. Burn the candle regularly at the same time every week until you meet again.

In addition, try the following nine Cruising altitude activities to further enhance feelings of togetherness with your partner.

9 Cruising altitude activities

1. Co-write a romance journal

The German composer Robert Schumann and his pianist virtuoso wife Clara Wieck shared a marriage journal for many years. Each week, they took turns being in charge of writing entries and responses to the other's previous entries. Their journal entries reflected the many ups and downs they endured over the course of their marriage until his untimely death.

Share a handwritten or electronic journal that conveys what you are going through. Write about your thoughts, feelings, fears, and hopes. Pass it back and forth on a regular basis so that you both have a chance to reply to each other's entries and write new entries. Sharing a journal will help you know and understand the other better, as well as interweave each other's thoughts and emotions. And later, when you are finally together, it will serve as a testament to your strength and courage.

2. Drink from love goblets

Buy mugs with each other's name imprinted on them and keep each other's mug. Or, buy a pair of mugs and have your best couple's photo imprinted on them. Synchronize the time when you drink the same hot beverage every morning.

3. Share cross words

Work on the same online or paper crossword puzzle at the same time every day. Use Instant Messaging to give each other hints.

4. Link forward

Forward links to fun places you would like to take each other, like an art museum, a romantic travel destination, or a trendy restaurant.

5. Fly around the world

Have you ever attended an around-the-world party? This kind of progressive party entails a network of hosts within a single community who provide snacks and refreshments in their homes according to a cultural theme. Globetrot around the world with your traveling partner by visiting international chat rooms online together.

6. Take a cyberholiday

Plan a dream cybertrip together, or both of you plan a surprise trip for the other. Begin your cybertrip by choosing your travel destination, a lodging, an excursion, lunch (include links to the restaurant and menu), and so on. In an email, paste and assemble the links to each site in the order you envision spending the day together. If possible, visit the sites online together at a designated time.

7. Share a cybermeal

Plan a cybermeal for a special occasion. Take a digital photo of the meal you have cooked, and send the photo as well as the link of the recipe, promising to prepare this for him or her when you are together. Alternatively, cook and eat the same meal at the same time, or at your same respective times. Two good recipe sites are www.epicurious.com and www.allrecipes.com.

8. Cross webcam paths

Check if your city has a live streaming webcam set up overlooking an accessible public area, or if you are traveling, see if your destination has public webcams. After you locate a public webcam, forward your mate the URL link and tell him or her when to visit the site (taking into account time zone difference). At the assigned meeting time, stand in front of the webcam holding flowers or a large greeting sign, or call your mate on your cell phone while he or she watches you.

9. Build a webpage or blogsite

Create a free webpage or blogsite together. Many people find blogsites easier to set up and maintain than websites. Some blogsites are free as well, such as those provided by Google. Work on the blogsite at the same time if possible or take turns adding something to it each week until you are reunited. Include a countdown ticker, calendar, maps and pictures of your locations, photos or a link to a shared online photo album, poems, a list of reasons why you love each other, and links to your favorite sites. Share a cyberjournal on your site to keep abreast of the daily events in each other's lives.

12. In-flight meal: Nurture the old-fashioned way

Ladies and gentlemen, our flight attendants are passing around the cabin to offer you a choice of meals and beverages.

The In-flight meal chapter helps you to nurture each other by offering nineteen ideas for making simple, creative gifts tailored to each other's uniqueness.

In the following pages are listed nineteen down-to-earth, fundamental ways of staying connected with your loved one.

19 simple yet creative ways to strengthen your bond

1. Write by hand

Handwritten letters are so underrated, and it's unfortunate that they have taken the back seat to the more impersonal email form of correspondence. It is hard to beat that warm and tantalizing feeling of your partner's handwritten postcard or letter tucked away in the breast pocket of your jacket close to your heart.

Handwriting lends a familiarity and physical dimension to an intimate letter that is lacking in email. Also, handwriting is better at evoking mood and personality. Choose the paper and ink that best reflects your mood and intention. As you write, keep each other's photo in view and anticipate how your words will affect your partner.

2. Use paper that reflects your routine

Do not limit yourself to only using stationery for writing special letters. Be innovative. You can personalize your letters even more by finding paper that reflects your every day surroundings. Write on anything including the placemats, paper menus, coasters, or napkins from the café where you have coffee, or the restaurant where you eat lunch. Write a letter on a handout from work or school or on a flyer from your neighborhood market. Have a set of pre-addressed and pre-stamped envelopes at your desk to help you stay disciplined in maintaining regular handwritten correspondence.

If you live in different countries, write a letter on the back of a placemat from a fast food restaurant. It might be interesting for your mate to see how the language, food products, and advertisement differ from his or her own. Plus, it comes free with lunch.

3. Personalize your correspondence

Use different color pens, stickers, magazine cut-outs, and attractive postage stamps to brighten up letters, postcards, envelopes, and packages. Personalize the envelope with funny or inspirational messages and cartoons.

4. Sweeten your correspondence

Express mail freshly baked cookies along with a romantic letter.

5. Inundate each other with postcards

Keep a constant stream of postcards going between you. Postcards make it easy to fill up the white space with a few words and doodles and don't cost much to mail. To facilitate regular correspondence, assemble a mixed bunch of pre-stamped postcards so that it's convenient to send one out at any time. However, remember to balance out postcards with occasional meaningful letters.

6. Vary your postcard themes

Collect and send an assortment of postcard themes including classic black and white celebrity photos, town and country depictions, and ones that are funny, stupid, artistic, or sentimental. Personalize them by doodling on both sides and affixing interesting postage stamps.

7. Send your message in parts

In the 1950s, Burma shaving cream was known for its innovative advertising campaign, posting one part of a message on a billboard at a time every half mile along American highways until the message was complete. In the spirit of Burma Shave, send one word or phrase on a postcard at a time every couple days until the message is complete.

8. Do-it-yourself

Draw or paint your own postcards on postcard-size art paper. Choosing colors and a medium that fit your mood, draw or paint a common setting typical to your every day life. Or, glue a photo onto a piece of poster board or balsa wood. Send your postcard in an envelope if you are concerned about privacy or about it getting ruined.

9. Scintillate

Scent your cards and letters with cologne and incense, or swathe a handful of aromatic blossoms between the pages.

10. Bookmark it

Put aside the last postcard you received from your mate and take it with you wherever you go. Keep it tucked in your shirt pocket or bag, or use it as a bookmark.

Case study: Robert, writer

In many respects, the LDR harkens back to the medieval days of courting. You pour all your energy into writing to your partner, exchanging gifts, and spending months or years getting to know him or her better. After all that, you may unite, and that's when the physical aspect of the relationship begins. At this point, the relationship will be stronger since you will know by then that you truly want to be with that other person.

11. Send clippings

Share your dreams and goals by sending each other clippings in the mail, or by forwarding links or attachments. Here are some examples of items you might enjoy sharing with each other.

- News or magazine articles according to each other's interests, studies, or work.

- An advertisement featuring your dream car, hairstyle, pet, house interior, or travel destination.

- Real estate clippings of your dream house.

- Short love stories or poems.

- Each other's horoscopes.

- Bizarre news items.

- Cartoons. White out the bubbles and write your own dialog.

12. Pen a poem

Write a poem on a scroll of parchment. Think about the first time you saw your mate, or the moment you realized you were falling in love. Write about one of your partner's special qualities, such as his or her smile, laugh, eyes, a movement, or scent.

Write a poem or a list of your mate's qualities based on the letters of his or her name. If you are feeling whimsical, write a limerick about one or both of you.

13. Write a comic strip

Draw a comic strip of you two in a true or fictional setting, doing and saying your typical quirky things. Or, write a cartoon about a funny occurrence your partner once told you.

14. Scrap it

Save every scrap of memorabilia when you spend time together. Later, when you are at home alone, assemble a small scrapbook and present it during your next visit. Include items such as photos, ticket stubs, menus or coasters, brochures of events, and the napkin you scribbled on together in the restaurant. Include the label of a special bottle of wine you shared. Personalize your scrapbook by doodling and writing messages around the items.

15. Achtung 2

Fashion an Advent calendar using your own materials and goodies. Sew or glue several pockets onto a flannel cloth. Enclose a small surprise into each pocket before stitching them shut.

16. Serenade

If you are musically inclined, record a love song or an instrumental and title it your mate's name. Sing about your feelings, how the season reminds you of him or her, or about how you met. Or, set an inspirational poem to music. If you simply like to sing, record yourself singing karaoke songs.

17. Reproduce

Draw, paint, sculpt, or create a mosaic in your partner's likeness from a photo, memory, or feeling.

18. Sketch

Interpret an inspirational love poem or song with a drawing or painting.

19. Be an artisan

Visit a craft shop where you can paint and fire ceramics. Make a mug with your mate's name painted on it. Or, try making something personal at home. There are many arts and crafts websites that explain how to make things such as homemade candles, soap, paper, dream catchers, and scrapbooks.

13. Duty-free shopping: Bond with simple technology

Ladies and gentlemen, our flight attendants are coming around with duty-free shopping carts for all your purchasing needs.

The chapter Duty-free shopping provides you with eighteen activities that will help deepen your bond by using simple and affordable communication technology, including phones, answering machines, email, and fax.

18 ways to connect with your partner using common technology

1. Give a ring

When you are running short of time to talk on the phone, call and let it ring only once so that your partner knows it's you and that you're thinking of him or her. Agree upon a phone ringing code in advance. Your partner can take this a step further and call you back, also letting it ring only once.

2. Send it through the grapevine

Let a friend begin the conversation by calling your mate for you. Have that friend praise your latest accomplishments and say how devoted you are. This is a good way for your mate to become acquainted with your friends and see another side of you through someone else's eyes.

3. Stay in the moment

Call your partner on your way to school or work. Talk with him or her while walking down the street or sitting in a coffee shop. It may be interesting for your partner to hear you in your surroundings, especially if you live in different cultures.

4. Maintain landline etiquette

Whenever you use the house phone, make sure you hang up gently after saying goodbye. Slamming down a phone is like slamming a door behind you. Often it is those first and last seconds of an intimate phone call that echo through a person's mind for the rest of the day.

Tip: Keep your mate's picture in view to avoid sounding flat and mechanical when doing anything that involves using your voice including phoning, recording a voice email, or recording a tape letter.

5. Picture the routine

Show glimpses of your daily life to make your partner feel as though he or she is right by your side. Throughout the day, use your digital or mobile phone camera to send pictures you take of romantic things, places, or yourself along with an audio file.

6. Videophone

Videophones are expensive, and if you don't have access to a computer and webcam and have the money, the sound and picture quality may be worth it. You may wish to first educate yourself about videophones on the Vialta website, and then see if you can get them cheaper on an auction website such as Ebay. On the Vialta website, a new pair of Beamer TV videophones cost $300 per pair and easily hook up to the TV.

7. Instant replay

Start the day or evening right. Replay his or her latest answering machine message upon waking up in the morning or going to bed at night to soothe yourself and stay connected.

8. Inspire love

You want your mate to know you are thinking about him or her, but do not have time or money for a phone conversation. Surprise your mate by leaving a message on the answering machine before he or she gets home from work. Say what you were doing, or what song you were listening to that moved you to think about him or her. Then hang up gently.

9. Be outgoing

If you are expecting your mate to call and leave a message on your machine, greet him or her with a personalized outgoing message. Play a romantic song in the background or record your outgoing message while doing something mundane like washing dishes so that he or she can catch a glimpse into your daily home life.

10. Be a serial messenger

Leave a series of short upbeat messages, play a song, or sing along to the radio on each other's answering machine whether or not the other is at home. Agree on a phone ringing code system beforehand so that you know when to not pick up the phone.

11. Hire a cheering squad

If you are a newer couple and are surrounded by supportive friends, have one of your friends call your partner. Let your friends pass the phone around so that everyone has a chance to take a few seconds to say something good about you. This allows your mate to know your friends better, as well as learn more about you from a different angle.

12. The three golden email rules

There are three things you should do before sending an email to your partner, especially if you are a new couple or speak different languages. Those three things are de-ironize, proofread, and personalize.

I. De-ironize

Email and Instant Messenger are great for immediacy, but their main problem, besides lacking a personal quality, is that irony and sarcasm do not translate well in cyberspace and are easily misunderstood.

II. **Proofread**

You have just whipped out a fun and loving email. Unfortunately, speedy typing usually means many typing errors. Your mate deserves that one minute of proofreading before sending your message. Avoid confusion and potential misunderstandings by checking for typos, spelling mistakes, and accidentally omitted words.

III. **Personalize**

After preventative damage has been done, choose a font that reflects your feelings or mindset. Consider using personalized email settings such as background or font color to emphasize mood and intention. Some people use emoticons to underscore their feelings and intentions. Alternatively, you could briefly summarize your thoughts and intentions at the end of important paragraphs to ensure your partner understands your point.

13. Recite

Send a voice email or leave an answering machine message with a twist. Recite a bit of poetry, sing a song, or read your partner's promising horoscope to him or her.

14. Make a discovery quest

Check your compatibility. Most relationship experts claim that the more compatible a couple is, the less chance there is for conflict later on after the initial excitement has dissipated. Take turns emailing questions to each other from a relationship-building question book that helps friends and couples get to know each other better.

15. Exchange email trivia

Take turns each week asking a few trivia questions in an email so that one of you must search the web for the answers. The trivia questions can be random or according to a theme such as music or sports.

16. Send an ecard

On special days, or days leading up to a special occasion, send several ecards from an ecard site such as Hallmark.com. In each card, write only a couple of words so that your mate has to read each of your ecards to receive the whole message.

17. Print transcripts

Print out all your email correspondence or bring your disk to a photocopier to have your emails bound into a keepsake book.

18. Fax it

If you both have access to a fax machine, scribble a quick love note written in a playful code, send a photocopy of an intriguing article, draw a cartoon of something funny that happened to you earlier in the day, or write a love letter. Let each other know if you share the fax machine with others, and use encoded language if necessary.

14. In-flight entertainment: Use high-technology

Ladies and gentlemen, in a few moments we will show you our feature film. Please sit back, relax, and enjoy the rest of the flight.

The In-flight entertainment chapter shows how you can use any high-tech communication items you might have to interweave your lives together and make yourselves feel more immediate and familiar to each other.

Make a tape letter

There is a wide variety of tape letters you can create, including recording yourself talking, making music compilations, and combining those two plus a number of other elements. Read on for discussion of devices you can use and ideas for creating your own unique tape letter.

MP3 player with voice recorder or Walkman cassette recorder

The MP3 player with voice recorder has replaced the audiotape Walkman cassette recorder within the realm of making voice recordings. However, for couples who don't have access to digital technology, the Walkman cassette recorder serves as a fine substitute.

Both are lightweight devices that effectively record quality voice and sound, making them perfect candidates for creating tape letters consisting of voice and music recordings. They are exceptionally useful for communicating indirectly when phoning is impossible due to clashing time zones or when you need to hear each other's voice at your own convenience. Furthermore, they are cheap; while many popular brands of a 1GB MP3 Player can be bought for under $100, the Sony cassette recorder costs $20 at Circuit City online.

More widely functional for making versatile tape letters, but heavier to handle, is a boom box that includes CD, MP3, radio, and dual tape recording.

If you are using an audiotape Walkman, you can transfer the audiotape contents onto a CD. To do this you need audio editing software and a firewire that can transfer data from your tape recorder to a PC.

Generally speaking, there are at least three main activities you can take part in by using your recorder. They are listed here from easy to more complicated.

1. Compile music

Download and burn your favorite love songs onto a CD to show your feelings. Decorate the shell case with loving words, drawings, or scanned images. Include the song titles, artists, and lyrics with the recording.

2. Compose digital voice letters

In addition, send your voice recordings on email as attachments, or save up your voice recordings by burning them onto a CD and send them out regularly.

3. Create a talking tape letter

Record yourself talking to your partner while getting ready for work or school, running errands, or at night in bed before falling asleep. The purpose of the tape letter is to draw your partner closer to you by using the personal effect of your voice, interweaved with songs that reflect your state of mind. The tape letter brings a sense of immediacy and familiarity with it, making your partner feel more connected to you, as if you are sitting right there next to him or her.

In your tape letters you can make observations, express opinions, and share your thoughts and feelings. Make it fun to listen to by incorporating a variety of topics you are interested in such as people, events, stories, poems, news, and music. Show different energy levels and sides of your personality. Make your depth of fondness for your mate apparent in your words, actions, and interactions with others. The recording of your tape letter may take place over the course of several days. Here are some basic steps to consider when making a tape letter.

Before making your tape letter

- Write a general list of topics you want to discuss.

- Choose the songs you want to play.

- Think in terms of 5- to 10-minute recording chunks.

- For each chunk, choose a few items from the general list of topics you want to talk about.

- Arrange topic chunks and songs so that the tape letter flows smoothly.

- Select a photo of your mate for you to focus on while recording your voice.

Topics

Before you begin recording your tape letter, look at the lists of possible tape letter topics below, ranging from conversation to music and beyond, that you can include in your talking tape letter.

Light topics

- Your interests.

- Your current endeavor, such as eating lunch or taking a walk.

- Errands you must do today or this week.

- Your daily life.

- Movies and books.

- Current local or international news events.

- Your school or job.

- Family and friends.

- Interesting surroundings.

- Future upcoming decisions or events.

- Your next reunion.

- Qualities you admire in your mate.

- Stories about your past.

- Amusing current stories and jokes.

Heavy topics

- Your previous reunion.

- Problems or concerns you may be experiencing or anticipating in your relationship.

- Your final reunion.

- Your short- and long-term goals.

- Your values.

- Significant moments in your life.

- Most influential people in your life.

- How much your partner means to you.

- Areas in your life you are trying to improve.

Music

- Record a song mix of new or old love songs.

- Record your favorite songs from each decade or genre.

- If your languages differ, exchange a compilation of romantic oldies.

- Request a song dedication from a radio station and record it when it broadcasts.

- Find and record a romantic song for each letter of your mate's name or pet name.

- Sing and record karaoke songs. Get the bar room crowd to join you in singing a cheesy love song.

- Write and play an original ballad. Or, if a poem inspires you, interpret it with music.

- Record his or her favorite radio programs.

Out and about

- Introduce family members and friends. Have them comment on you, your character, or what's going on with your life, or have them share encouraging words regarding your relationship.

- Chat with friends.

- Attend fun or important events.

- Do mundane stuff like driving around, cooking dinner, sitting on the patio, or listening to music.

- Record the sounds of your town as you run errands. Make passing remarks about the people and things you see.

Language learners

- Record radio news briefs and commercials on the radio over the course of several days. Then summarize them or add your thoughts so that your mate can learn more about your opinions on topics that interest you.

- Read interesting short newspaper or magazine articles.

- Make a tapebook like the audiobooks you can buy in the store. Read aloud from your favorite children's book, chapter by chapter. Send the book with the tapebook so that your partner can read along.

After you have selected your topics and music, you are now ready to begin making your tape letter. Although it's helpful to base your tape letters on a standard formula, there is no rigid formula you must use. However, the following is a simple formula you may want to use to help you get started. Attempt to vary this formula each time you record a tape letter to keep them interesting.

While making your tape letter
- Place your partner's picture in front of you while recording your voice.

- Start the tape letter with a song or two to set the mood with music that expresses how you feel about your mate.

- Greet your partner, state the date and time, and say what you're doing so that he or she can visually place you and your location.

- Discuss a few of your chosen topics.

- Bid farewell, perhaps describing the next set of songs you are about to play before ending the day's recording session.

Make sure you also…

- Alternate between talking and playing music every five to ten minutes.

- Vary your talking locations for each voice recording.

- Show your different sides: playful, romantic, serious, casual, and quirky.

As a rule, record all the things on your tape letter that you would like your mate to be present for. Also, keep your mate's emotional needs in mind regarding the time he or she will be listening to your tape letter. For example, if your mate is about to take final exams, be extra supportive.

Tip: If you are using a Walkman, use the pause button rather than the stop button to end each recording session. It's easier on the listener's ears and helps the recording sessions flow together more smoothly.

After making your tape letter

- Decorate the shell case with encouraging words, doodles, drawings, or scanned images.

- Make sure you include all the song titles and lyrics, poems, or articles you used in your recordings.

Camera

If feeling visually close is one of your number one goals, then you are going to need a reliable camera. These days there is a variety of affordable cameras to choose from. Digital cameras are great for instant viewing by attaching images to email, creating an online photo album, posting pictures on a website or blogsite, or snail mailing printouts. Polaroid instamatic cameras have recently made a comeback, now generating wallet-sized pictures, while most disposable cameras these days take pictures with fine color and resolution. Exchange pictures frequently to enhance feelings of familiarity.

On the following pages are four main areas with ideas for capturing unique pictures of you, your surroundings, and the special and ordinary moments in your life.

Area #1: Places

- Places where you shared romantic moments, or where you would like to take him or her in the future.

- Your house, campus, work, and hangouts.

- The different angles of your bedroom.

- The rooms in your house including where you email or talk on the phone. Pin up each other's photos in the corresponding rooms of your houses.

- A romantic setting such as you sitting in the bathtub full of soap bubbles surrounded by candles.

- The view from your bedroom or living room window.

- Ordinary street scenes in your city.

- Interesting architecture or vistas in your town.

- Outside during different seasons. For example, make a snowman that resembles you, hold out a spring rosebud, or write a message in the park with newly fallen leaves.

Area #2: Events

- Festivals.
- Parties.
- Concerts.
- Sports tournaments.

Area #3: People

- Your baby pictures.
- Family and friends.
- Co-workers.
- People you deal with daily, such as the corner grocer guy.

Area #4: Personal

- Photos of you exercising, dressed up, being goofy, or looking romantic.

- A picture of you in the outfit he or she likes best on you or is most familiar with, such as the one you were wearing when you first met.

- A wallet-sized photo of you being romantic, silly, or serious. Hold up a large greeting sign, a flower, or your partner's favorite dessert.

- For important days, hold a sign with a special message wishing a happy birthday or good luck.

- Pick a favorite photo of you two together and frame one for each of you or get it imprinted on a pair of key chains, mouse pads, mugs, fridge magnets, placemats, or t-shirts. Many online photo album websites and photo shops offer this service.

Tip: Send a photo every time you send a letter or card.

Below are several more fun ideas for helping to keep abreast of each other's daily lives.

Portrait puzzle

Have your favorite couple's photo made into a puzzle at a photo shop or album website. Send the whole puzzle at one time or a couple pieces at a time.

Digital journey

Create a digital photograph timeline highlighting your most precious moments together. Or, create a parallel timeline for both of you beginning with infancy. Publish the digital timeline onto an online photo album site or personal website. You could also make a hard copy photo timeline using snapshots or scanned images.

Update

Send current photos often to keep each other updated on the daily changes in each other's appearance.

Shrine

Dedicate one section of your wall to your partner with a collection of his or her best photos as well as couple's photos, postcards, and memorabilia. Rotate items as your collection increases.

Frame your day

Keep a framed picture of your partner next to your bed so that he or she is the first and last person you see every day. Set your favorite digital picture of your partner as wallpaper on your screensaver.

Scan it

Scan photos or art and send them as email attachments or post them onto your website.

VHS / DVD player

If you live on different continents and plan to exchange videos or DVDs, make sure your VHS or DVD player has multi-region reading capability, as player frequencies vary. Below is a list of activities you can try using your player.

- Record your mate's favorite TV shows.

- Watch video letters you make for each other.

- Send new or used video films.

- Watch films simultaneously or according to time zone.

Part V Descent: Safe in the Loading Dock

15. A smooth landing: Epilogue

Ladies and gentlemen, we hope you had a pleasurable flight and wish you an enjoyable stay. Thank you for flying with LDR Airlines.

We began our journey with my describing to you the kinds of problems I was facing in my seven-year LDR, as well as problems my friends who were in LDRs were experiencing. These problems seemed formidable at the time, but I believed long distance relationships could be made more manageable somehow. This prompted me to interview and survey couples in long distance relationships with the goal of writing a practical and inspirational book that would help these determined yet vulnerable committed couples thrive during the long stretches of time spent apart.

Many of the positive ideas and activities that are included in this book are things that helped my LDR last as long as it did. Indeed, the ideas and activities included in this book, as well as the love and admiration my partner and I felt for each other, made our relationship extraordinary. On a more somber note, many of the topics in the Layover and Turbulence chapters are also things I learned from that relationship.

As a result, I learned as much about being in an LDR as a result of it being successful as well as unsuccessful. It was successful because I will always treasure the happy memories of being in that special relationship. However, by society's standards, it was unsuccessful because our relationship ended. Even though that particular LDR did not work out as I had hoped at the time, I firmly believe that LDRs can and do succeed with a lot of hard work, some practical guidance, and a little good luck. As for my own story, everything has worked out for the best. We are both happily married, yet to someone else, and have children with our spouses.

Everyone has different beliefs on how to maintain and strengthen a long distance bond. For me, constant involvement in each other's lives was integral to feeling close. In addition, sending simple self-made gifts and synchronizing special moments and our routines intensified the feelings of love, excitement, and joy I felt from being with my partner. What matters most is that you find ways to nurture your bond that add to your happiness and desire to stay together.

I would like to invite you to share your own long distance relationship experiences and activity ideas with me. Whether you have had good or bad experiences, or a mixture of both, I'd love to hear from you. And of course, I would like to hear if *The Long Distance Relationship Guidebook* has helped in any way to make your relationship a more comfortable and rewarding experience.

Please email me at:

www.lulu.com/sylviashipp

Submissions cannot be returned and become the property of *The Long Distance Relationship Guidebook.*

About the author

Sylvia Shipp is an author and researcher, university teacher, wife and a mother of two boys. As a long distance relationship expert, Sylvia began conducting interviews and surveys on long distance relationships more than a decade ago. Once her own seven-year LDR ended, she decided to put the pain to good use and began writing *The Long Distance Relationship Guidebook*, a comprehensive, practical, and easy-to-read book on maintaining long distance relationships that would help other committed LDR couples thrive. Meanwhile, a couple years later she began her second long-distance relationship that resulted in marriage and two beautiful sons.

Aside from endeavoring in writing fiction and non-fiction, Sylvia teaches English as a foreign language at a university in the Persian Gulf. When she isn't teaching, she and her family travel or spend time at their home in western Pennsylvania.

LaVergne, TN USA
13 September 2009
157719LV00003B/14/A